Attracting & Feeding
BLUEBIRDS

Stan Tekiela

T0161893

Adventure Publications
Cambridge, Minnesota

Dedication

To Agnieszka Bacal for her passion and love for nature, especially bluebirds.

Acknowledgments

Many thanks to the All Seasons Wild Bird Stores in Minnesota, which have been instrumental in obtaining some of the images in this book.

Credits

Front and back cover photos of birds by Stan Tekiela. Front cover pattern by EVAsr/Shutterstock. Front cover bird icon by SaveJungle/Shutterstock

All photos by Stan Tekiela except for pg. 11 (Western female) by Sundry Photography/Shutterstock.
All full- and half-page bird images are of Eastern Bluebirds unless otherwise labeled.

Edited by Sandy Livoti

Cover and book design by Jonathan Norberg

10 9 8 7 6 5 4 3 2

Attracting & Feeding Bluebirds
First Edition 2017
Second Edition 2022
Copyright © 2017 and 2022 by Stan Tekiela
Published by Adventure Publications
An imprint of AdventureKEEN
310 Garfield Street South
Cambridge, Minnesota 55008
(800) 678-7006
www.adventurepublications.net
ISBN 978-1-64755-329-6 (pbk.); ISBN 978-1-64755-330-2 (ebook)

TABLE OF CONTENTS

All About Bluebirds

Of all the wonderful birds that share our backyards, the bluebird seems to attract the highest praise. Through the years many poets and writers have expounded upon this blue beauty. Henry David Thoreau said, "The bluebird carries the sky on his back." Indeed, it does!

My attraction to bluebirds extends to over 30 years of hosting a nesting trail that has about 60 bluebird nest boxes. In most years I fledge over 100 chicks, and I get great satisfaction from helping these marvelous birds.

Three bluebird species occur in the United States and Canada. The Eastern Bluebird (*Sialia sialis*) is found in the eastern two-thirds of the country and southern Canada. The Mountain Bluebird (*Sialia currucoides*) lives in the western half of the country and extends into Canada and Alaska. The Western Bluebird (*Sialia mexicana*) is the look-alike cousin of the Eastern and is seen in all of our western states and beyond.

Bluebirds are in a very large group of perching birds (passerines) called the thrush family (Turdidae). Eastern and Western Bluebirds are similar to the most famous thrush family member, the American Robin. They all have rusty red chests, white bellies and similar shapes.

I always look forward to the return of the bluebirds each spring. In many regions, these tough and hardy birds stick around in autumn well after all the other migratory birds have left, right up to the time snow begins to fall.

male

female

FACTS

Relative Size: the Eastern Bluebird is smaller than an American Robin

Length: 7–8" (18–20 cm)

Wingspan: 12–13" (30–33 cm)

Weight: 1.1 oz. (31 g)

Male: deep blue head, back, wings and tail, an orange to rusty red chin, chest and flanks, a white belly, black legs and feet and a small, thin dark bill

Female: similar to male but duller blue, sometimes appearing gray, with a dull red chin, chest and flanks

Juvenile: similar to female except overall duller, often with white spots throughout, white throat with dark vertical lines

Nest: cavity, old woodpecker hole or man-made nest box; female builds nest with dried grasses or pine needles, lining the nest with soft, fine grasses

Migration: partial to complete migrator; leaves late in the fall and returns early in spring

Food: insects, fresh fruit, dried fruit; readily comes to feeders that offer mealworms

RANGE & HABITAT

The Eastern Bluebird has the largest range of the bluebird species. It lives in open grasslands, prairies, park-like settings and along forest edges, preferring wide-open spaces with few trees. It has adapted well to human activity, nesting in parks and backyards alike and often sharing the habitat with House Wrens and Tree Swallows.

The ranges of Mountain and Western Bluebirds are shown on pages 10–11. The Mountain Bluebird is much more widespread and common than the Western. During breeding season, the Mountain Bluebird is in open meadows and fields up to 12,000 feet in elevation. It winters in lower elevations in meadows, prairies and hedgerows with sparse shrubs and small trees.

The Western Bluebird lives at the edge of open wood-lands and is often associated with coniferous forests, particularly Ponderosa Pine. It likes disturbed habitats, such as areas with many dead trees left from forest fires. It also likes pinyon-juniper forests.

Maps represent all bluebird species in the United States and Canada.

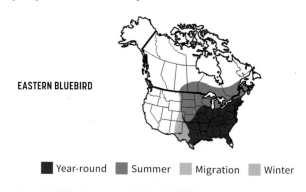

EASTERN BLUEBIRD

■ Year-round ■ Summer ■ Migration ■ Winter

MOUNTAIN BLUEBIRD

male

female

Year-round Summer Migration Winter

WESTERN BLUEBIRD

male

female

Year-round　　Summer　　Migration　　Winter

11

SONGS & CALLS

All of our bluebird species sing gracefully, pleasing us with their wonderful songs. They aren't loud or powerful singers, but what they lack in volume, they make up with a richly complex repertoire of delicate chortles.

Before selecting a mate, the males tend to perch high up and sing to defend their territory from other males. Sometimes they even give songs in flight. This broadcasts far and wide their warning to steer clear.

To attract a mate, the male sings an advertisement warble from a low perch. Unlike many other birds that tilt back their heads, fling open their bills and belt out their songs, bluebirds are more composed and sing as if they were doing it under their breath. They hardly open their bills to allow their delicate songs to escape.

After pairs are formed, the males tend to sing much softer songs from their low perches. Their amazing songs last about 2–3 seconds and consist of several parts strung together to make complete songs.

Quick-Tips

- Male Eastern Bluebirds sing a low-pitched song of a few micro phrases strung together, making a complete song that lasts about 2–3 seconds

- Studies show that males with more diverse micro songs attract more females

- Sometimes the male's scolding call is much louder than his advertisement song

- Bluebirds are well known to sing with their beaks closed

- It's not uncommon to hear bluebirds singing their songs all year long

Female Eastern Bluebirds also sing, but they do so much less frequently and much more softly. When a female sees a predator entering the territory, she will call out. Females are much more free with their warning calls than with their songs.

Bluebird calls are short, nonmusical notes that are used to show displeasure or to warn other birds and predators that they have been spotted. Calls last less than a second, with the male calls lasting slightly longer than those of the females. Their call sounds as if they are saying "chit-chit-chit."

Unlike some other birds, bluebirds sing and give calls all year long. They do this to keep in contact without having to look for one another.

male

female

BLUEBIRD NESTS & HOUSES

Bluebirds build simple cup nests in both natural and man-made cavities. Nesting in cavities tends to be safer than in open cup nests. A cavity provides protection from the weather and also from some predators.

However, bluebirds lack the ability to excavate their own cavities. They either have to find a natural cavity in a tree or rely on other birds, such as woodpeckers, that have already excavated, used and evacuated a nesting hole.

Fortunately, bluebirds take to man-made nest boxes very easily. Many different styles of nest boxes have been developed over the past decades. Some of the most common varieties that work the best to house our blue friends are shown in this chapter.

Natural Cavities

Bluebirds have nested in natural cavities for thousands of years. After gas-powered chain saws were invented, people became efficient at removing dead trees, but this produced a problem for bluebirds. They were nearly killed off in the early to mid-1900s due to lack of nesting cavities and habitat, along with widespread overuse of pesticides. Many organizations formed to help restore the populations, and they are doing much better now.

Natural cavities still provide bluebirds with many nesting opportunities, but not as much as in the past. Today, only a small percentage of all bluebirds in the United States and Canada nest in natural cavities, with more doing so in the western half of the country.

Bluebird Nests

Once a cavity is selected, the female does the majority of the nest construction. It takes her about 8–12 days to build a nest, depending on the availability of nesting material and the cooperation of the weather. Males will occasionally bring in some nesting material.

Nests are typically made with dried grasses and are in the basic shape of a cup. Occasionally bluebirds use pine needles or sometimes animal fur or hair in the construction. There's not much weaving or complexity, and the female uses her body to contour the cup.

Man-Made Nest Boxes

Man-made bluebird nest boxes have been designed, tested and proven not only to help bluebirds nest more efficiently, but also to help deter predators and reduce the chances that other bird species will use the houses.

Often the style of nest box is a matter of preference by the person who is monitoring the birds. Several things need to be considered. Most important is the ease of opening the box to check the occupants. Easy access to inspect the birds or clean the box is very important.

Studies show that bluebirds hatched in a particular style of nest box often prefer the same box style when they start a family of their own. So, choosing several different styles may not be good when you are selecting boxes for a bluebird nesting trail. Pick one style or perhaps two and stick with it.

If you build a bluebird house, it's very important to pick the best quality of wood, such as rough-cut cedar, for construction. Use wood that's at least ¾-inch thick. This helps provide insulation against cold and heat. Do not use plywood, which delaminates, or treated woods, because the chemicals may adversely affect the birds. Ventilation holes are vital if you live where temperatures go above 90°F regularly. Follow construction directions exactly, but painting the box exterior is not necessary. Bluebirds don't nest in painted trees, so make your nest box au naturel as well.

Several commercially produced bluebird box styles are excellent in quality, with superior wood. Because others are extremely poor quality, be particular when buying nest boxes from the store.

The NABS Eastern/Western Bluebird nest box is a simple square box with a slanted roof, and a door that opens on one side. It's sold at many stores, and detailed construction plans are also available online or at your local bluebird society. The front of the box has a small, round entrance hole 1½ inches in diameter. Oftentimes this nest box can be cut from one length of board.

In certain parts of the country, the Peterson-style bluebird house is very popular and has proven to be great for nesting bluebirds. This house has a slanted front entrance with a large sloping roof. Due to the angles, extra care must be taken during construction—although the job isn't as hard as it looks. Just be sure to install the floor so the surface is flat. I've seen even seasoned woodworkers make the mistake of slanting the floor.

The Gilbertson nest box is different from the others, as it is made from PVC pipe. This box does well at keeping out some predators and reducing use by sparrows and other species. It can last a long time, but taking the

PVC nesting chamber off and putting it back on can be tricky. This box is good in high-traffic areas, because it can be moved fairly easily.

Predator guards can be very helpful in regions where skunks, raccoons, domestic cats, snakes and more are feeding on baby bluebirds. There are two main kinds of predator guards.

One type of guard is a round metal pipe that fits over the post holding the nest box. These are similar to squirrel guards for bird feeders, and they're especially good at keeping snakes away. They also help deter mice, squirrels and raccoons that try to climb the pole.

A metal wire mesh guard is another popular option. Many people put mesh guards around the entrance holes of their bluebird nest boxes. Bluebirds don't have any issues navigating through these devices, but the mesh will stop raccoons and house cats from reaching fully into the boxes to get the eggs or chicks within. These guards work well and are highly recommended.

Placing Nest Boxes

Putting bluebird boxes on trees invites squirrels and mice to move in and take over, leaving your bluebirds no place to nest. The best plan of action is to mount the nest box on a short metal pole so the box is 4–6 feet off the ground. Metal poles help prevent snakes, raccoons, squirrels and other predators from climbing up. Nest boxes on poles should be placed in open areas away from shrubs and trees. The closer the box is to woodlands, the higher the chance a House Wren will move in.

In nature, the entrance of a natural cavity or an old woodpecker hole faces any direction. Regardless, if you can place the box so the entrance isn't facing prevailing winds (often from the west), this could be best. Many people face their boxes south to help the birds warm up in the cool weather of early spring. However, during summer this isn't beneficial and can lead to overheating.

EGGS, CHICKS & JUVENILES

Eastern Bluebirds can nest two or sometimes three times per season, depending on the region. Babies hatch naked and helpless and can't regulate their own body temperature. The mother must continue to sit on them (brood) until they have enough feathers to keep warm, usually about 5–7 days. She leaves only to eat and defecate. Adults come and go to feed the chicks. At this stage, the male does most of the feeding.

Just over two weeks after hatching, the young are nearly the size of their parents. They have gray feathers with white spots and a white eye-ring around each eye. These juveniles leave the nest box (fledge) and sometimes land on the ground. If they make it to a small tree or shrub, they will fly up into the branches. Within days, they are following their parents around and fluttering their wings, begging for food. Parents lead them to feeders that offer some of their favorite foods, such as meal-worms and fruit.

Broods: up to 3 per season

Clutch Size: 4–5 eggs

Egg Length: .8–1" (2–2.5 cm)

Egg Color: pale blue without markings

Incubation: 12–14 days; female incubates

Hatchlings: naked except for sparse tufts of down feathers, with eyes and ears sealed shut

Fledging: 15–18 days

Mountain Bluebird

BLUEBIRD TRIVIA

- The bluebird is considered the international symbol of happiness.

- The social network Twitter uses a symbol of a bluebird as its logo.

- The Eastern Bluebird is the official state bird of New York and Missouri.

- The Mountain Bluebird is the official state bird of Idaho and Nevada.

- Bluebirds are some of the most coveted birds to attract and complement your garden.

- All species of bluebirds are insect eaters. They are welcomed by gardeners all over the United States and Canada.

- A bluebird's eyesight is tremendous! It can see a small insect from over 50 yards away.

- Bluebirds are able to eat the toxic Monarch Butterfly caterpillar by squeezing out the toxic insides before swallowing the remainder of the insect.

- You can attract bluebirds to your yard by offering trays with mealworms, dried fruit or suet.

- After the breeding season, small flocks of bluebirds gather to migrate and spend the winter together.

- Bluebirds are some of the few species that will sing their lovely chortling songs all year long.

Western Bluebird

Feeding Bluebirds

Bluebirds eat mainly insects in spring and summer, but they also eat fresh and dried fruit. In late summer, when insects are less plentiful, they eat fresh fruit on shrubs, vines and trees, including dogwood, mulberry, sumac, hackberry, raspberry, wild grape, holly, eastern red cedar, pokeweed and buckthorn. In fall and early winter, they enjoy the dried fruit left from the summer months.

Bluebirds normally eat insects on or near the ground. They sit on branches and dart out to snatch bugs. They like grasshoppers, caterpillars and other large insects. I have even seen some catch Chorus Frogs (¾-inch aquatic frogs) to eat and also to feed to their young.

The best way to attract bluebirds is with mealworms. Live mealworms are sold in plastic tub-like containers and should be stored in the refrigerator, where they can remain fresh for 1–2 months. A single bluebird can eat dozens of mealworms each day, so purchasing them in the hundreds or thousands is recommended.

Mealworms also are sold dried in plastic bag-like packages. This is the most economical way to buy them, and you can purchase thousands at a time. Some bluebirds, however, don't feed on mealworms unless they are alive and moving. You can start feeding your bluebirds with live mealworms, and after they get into a routine of visiting your feeder, you can switch to the dried mealworms.

Another surefire way to get bluebirds into your yard is to put out feeders with fresh or dried fruit. Raisins are a popular choice, as are dried cranberries. Small pieces of apple or banana also work. You can offer a selection of fruits in a dish with drainage holes in the bottom.

Suet feeders will attract bluebirds in early spring before insects become plentiful. Suet and insects are both a great source of protein. Some people crumble small bits of suet into their mealworm or fruit feeder. Many suet cakes come packed with insects. These make tasty and nutritious offerings for bluebirds.

Sunflower hearts are also a good source of nutrition for bluebirds when other food sources are scarce. The hearts are just the interior meat of sunflower seeds. Many species of birds will also be attracted to this food, and it can be offered in many standard seed feeders.

If you have bluebirds spending the winter in your area, you might want to consider offering these foods to help them eat hardily through the season.

LIVE & DRIED MEALWORMS

Mealworms: Mealworms are the worm-like larvae of darkling beetles (*Tenebrio molitor*)—grain beetles that are flightless. An excellent source of protein, calcium and vitamins, mealworms have about 13 percent fat and 21 percent protein. Offering mealworms will attract bluebirds as well as a variety of other species of birds that don't normally come to traditional seed feeders, such as American Robins and Gray Catbirds.

When bluebirds find mealworms, they gorge themselves! Live mealworms (shown on page 28) must be stored in a container from which they cannot escape. A steep container with slippery sides is essential and should be refrigerated. Offer dried mealworms (shown here) in a shallow tray.

FRESH & DRIED FRUITS

Fruits: Offering fresh fruit is a popular way to bring in bluebirds. Many fresh fruits, including berries, cherries, bananas, apples, melons and grapes, are good choices to put out.

Offering dried fruit is a another great way to draw bluebirds to your yard. Many dried fruits, such as currants, raisins, dates and prunes, are selections they will like.

SEEDS & LEGUMES

Hulled Sunflower Chips: Hulled sunflower is just the meat or nutmeat of the sunflower seed without the hard, inedible outer shell, and bluebirds enjoy it in pieces or chips. This option is also known by other names, depending on where you purchase it. Sunflower chips have 37 percent protein and are very high in fat.

Peanut Hearts: Pieces of peanuts, called peanut hearts, are another option to feed bluebirds. The peanut plant, *Arachis hypogaea*, is a member of the legume or bean family and grows underground. Peanuts contain 45 percent fat and 24 percent protein, and they are a good source of vitamins A and E as well as zinc, iron and potassium. Peanut hearts are popular in suet.

OTHER FOOD

Suet: Another way to attract bluebirds is to offer suet. Suet cakes are composed mainly of beef fat—specifically, fat from around the kidneys and loins. However, more and more suet is coming from fat anywhere on the cow.

Suet is an extremely high-energy food with a high calorie count, and bluebirds easily digest it. Some varieties are mixed with dried fruit, seeds or nuts. Suet in these forms is a great way to give your bluebirds an especially tasty treat.

Offer suet in specialized wire feeders with a bottom perch. These allow bluebirds to reach into the cake and break off small pieces. Protect all of your suet feeders from squirrels, chipmunks, raccoons and opossums, which will take the entire cake. You can also crumble up suet cakes into a mealworm tray for the bluebirds to grab while they're feeding on the mealworms.

STORING MEALWORMS

Storing mealworms is easy: simply keep them in a sealed plastic container. Most times, mealworms are packaged in containers that are already perfect for long-term storage.

Keep your mealworm container in a cool, dry place away from direct sunlight—inside your refrigerator is the best place. If you don't store the mealworms in the refrigerator, they will quickly morph into the pupal stage, which transforms into darkling beetles. Often, bluebirds do not like the pupal stage, when mealworms look like yellow to white maggots.

When you keep mealworms sealed in the refrigerator, they can last upwards of several months. I'm sure your bluebirds will eat the mealworms much faster, so long-term storage will never be a problem.

FEEDING Q&A

Why do bluebirds like mealworms so much?
Bluebirds are insect-eating birds and need to hunt for their meals. But this takes so much time and energy! Eating from a dish of mealworms is a fast way to obtain calories and an easy way to give food to their young.

Should I feed bluebirds during summer?
You can feed bluebirds at any time of year that you see them. During the lean months, when insects are not plentiful (early spring, fall and winter), bluebirds will be more eager to take your mealworm offerings. But they will also eat mealworms during summer, when they are feeding their babies. You can also put out dried

fruit at that time. Fresh fruit should be put out during the cooler times of the year.

When is it too late to put out feeders?

You can set out bluebird feeders anytime the birds are around. Putting feeders out even during the middle of summer can still attract bluebirds.

What if I leave town or take a vacation?

It's not true that when you start feeding bluebirds, you can't stop. Bluebirds do not become dependent on our feeders. They take advantage of the quick and easy offerings, but once those are gone they simply fly off to another feeder or a wild food source. When you get back home, just refill your feeders and watch the bluebirds return. It won't take long.

Should I stop feeding bluebirds at the end of summer?

Feeding bluebirds all summer long is one of the many highlights of summertime backyard bird feeding. Their bright plumages and cheerful songs are just a couple of the reasons why we feed them. Your offerings won't stop them from migrating, so there is no need to stop feeding them. Depending on where you live, one morning in late October or early November you will wake up and the bluebirds will be gone. The good news is you can look forward to their return the following spring.

I have a birdbath. What about mosquitoes?

Birdbaths are essential for most backyard feeding stations, but mosquito proliferation is a concern. There are products that release a larvicide, killing all mosquito larvae, but a much more natural solution is to prevent them from developing at all. Moving the water with a small waterfall or battery-powered water wiggler does this, or simply change the water. It takes about seven days for mosquito larvae to develop, so use your garden hose or a bucket once a week to keep them in check.

Water, even in winter?
Bluebirds always need water to drink, so a shallow offering anytime of the year is good. Heated birdbaths will attract many bluebirds in winter. If your birdbath is deep, add less water or a layer of small rocks to make it shallow. Water shouldn't be more than an inch or so deep, because drenched feathers will freeze quickly in extremely cold temperatures and ground the birds.

If a lot of bluebirds are visiting my feeders during winter, should I put out more?
Responding to changing feeding habits is the key to attracting and enjoying the bluebirds in your yard even more. If you notice more bluebirds showing up in winter, it's always good to put out more mealworm dishes, suet feeders, extra dried fruit and water to accommodate the additional visitors.

Bluebird Feeders

Offering the right foods is certain to attract bluebirds and keep them coming back. All three bluebird species come to feeders with mealworms or fruit.

There are many different kinds of feeders that can offer these favored foods. A mealworm feeder can be as simple as a glass bowl or plastic dish that contains a dozen or more mealworms. There are also many styles of decorative mealworm feeders available for purchase.

Homemade mealworm feeders work just as well as store-bought varieties, and they give you the added satisfaction of making them yourself. Some fancier types have entrance holes that force the birds to enter the feeder in order to snatch the mealworms. Bluebirds at these kinds of feeders are fun to watch.

Quick-Tips

- Some of the best feeders for bluebirds are simple ones that are easy to clean or replace if they break
- Specialized mealworm feeders that offer easy access to a small supply of mealworms are also good choices
- Large mealworm feeders with roofs will attract many bluebirds, but they need a little more work to clean
- Dried mealworms last a long time, and you can buy them by the thousands to offer in multiple feeders
- Use a squirrel baffle to keep unwanted critters from reaching the mealworms or fruit offerings

FEEDER TYPES

Mealworm Feeder: Usually plastic with tall sides. Material needs to be slippery so live mealworms can't crawl out. Many kinds of dishes and trays exist to feed bluebirds this treat. You can also recycle a plastic food container and fashion your own design.

Covered Mealworm Feeder: This feeder has a roof that provides protection from the weather and sun. It has small entrance holes, which restrict which bird species can access the mealworms.

Platform, Tray or Ground Feeder: Also known as a fly-through feeder. Usually has a flat, open surface for seeds. Hangs from a series of wires or chains, rests on a central post or pole, or sits on the ground with the bottom of the tray about 12 inches off the ground. Made of wood or metal and often has a series of holes or slots for water drainage. Some have a protective roof.

Window Feeder: Made of lightweight plastic or wood. Suction cups adhere these feeders to window surfaces, allowing for close viewing. Many types of foods, such as mealworms, fruit and seeds, can be used in window feeders.

Suet Feeder: A treated metal cage that holds a preformed cake of suet. Bluebirds feed easily from styles with a stand at the bottom for perching. Some have a roof, which sheds rainwater and accumulations of snow and protects the food from bird droppings. Suet feeders hang from a chain or pole, or attach to a post.

PLACING FEEDERS

Feeding bluebirds is fun and easy, so put feeders where you can easily enjoy them from within your home. They should be in areas near your home where you spend a lot of time, and close enough to a window where you can see outside clearly and comfortably.

Most feeding stations are approximately 20–40 feet away from the home. Placing feeders closer draws bluebirds to where you can watch them more easily. The closer the feeders, however, the more likely you will have window strikes.

Feeders close to shrubs or other cover give bluebirds a place to stage and look for predators before flying in to feed. Plant cover also gives them a quick place to hide in case a hawk swoops in. Feeders in the middle of large open spaces work well for bluebirds.

When placing feeders, be sure to install a squirrel or raccoon baffle on each one. Baffles are metal tubes that prevent these animals from climbing shepherd's hooks or poles and accessing the feeders.

Place bird feeders where squirrels can't jump onto or over the baffle. The basic placement rule is 5 feet and 8 feet—meaning feeders should be at least 5 feet off the ground and at least 8 feet from any other surface from which a squirrel can jump. This includes trees, houses, sheds, outdoor grills, birdbaths, patio furniture and anything else a squirrel can climb to get to the feeders.

Maintaining Feeders & Good Practices

Feeder maintenance is vital for the overall health of all birds. How often you clean your feeders depends on the weather and season. Cleaning is more important in summer than winter, and feeders in wet environments need more cleaning than those in dry climes. Feeders with foods high in oil content, such as suet, must be cleaned more often than those holding less fatty foods.

Mealworm feeders tend to stay fairly clean, but it's very important to clean feeders that are offering live food.

Bird feeders are the number one place where disease is spread. Dirty feeders hold bacteria, viruses and mold that can sicken or kill birds. Feeders are also a place where birds spread disease from one to another.

A number of transmissible diseases are associated with birds, including bluebirds, and their droppings. To be safe, use good hygiene practices and take some basic precautions when filling or cleaning your feeders.

For example, when you clean feeders, wear a pair of rubber gloves. You don't need to be gloved to fill the feeders, but after cleaning, vigorously wash your gloved hands and cleaning brushes with warm, soapy water. Use paper towels to pat dry, and discard the towels.

CLEANING YOUR FEEDERS

Always try to use rubber gloves when cleaning the feeding area, because there are several diseases that can be picked up from bird droppings. *Histoplasma capsulatum* is a fungus in soils that is deposited from bird and bat droppings. It is recommended to wear a particulate mask while raking up or blowing away seed hulls underneath feeders. Many people who contract histoplasmosis don't develop symptoms, but some exhibit mild flu-like symptoms. Rarely, some people can suffer serious complications.

Cryptococcosis is another fungal disease found in the environment, and it also comes from bird droppings. Often associated with pigeon droppings, it is best to wear rubber gloves and a mask when cleaning up scat on feeders and around roosting sites, attics, cupolas and other places where large numbers of birds gather. Like histoplasmosis, many people don't suffer any symptoms. Some just come down with symptoms of a mild flu.

West Nile virus is carried by mosquitoes. Bluebirds and other birds contract it but don't transfer it to humans, so there is no need to be concerned about getting this disease from your feeders.

Keeping your feeding station clean and refreshing the sites are quick and easy ways to stop the spread of avian disease and other diseases from bird droppings.

A quick dry-clean is recommended each time you refill your feeders. Dump out the old food before adding any new and knock out any clumps. Also, wipe down the feeder with a dry rag to remove the bird scat before refilling it.

You should wet-clean your feeder if there are obvious signs of mold or mildew. Dead birds near feeders or on them are another indicator that a major wet cleaning is needed. Use a sanitizing solution of one part bleach to nine parts warm water, or purchase a commercial bird feeder cleaning solution.

To remove bits of stuck food, use a scrub brush. Insert a long-handled bottlebrush in tubes, and use an old toothbrush to clean other hard-to-reach places.

Dismantle the feeder as much as possible and scour with your scrub brushes and cleaning solution. Clean inside and out and rinse well with hot water. Allow the feeder to dry thoroughly overnight, or lay the parts out in the sunlight before reassembling and refilling it.

Cleaning around the base of a feeding station is very important. Rake up or blow away old food debris on the ground. This will accumulate after a long winter or other extended feeding. Add or refresh any mulch or gravel beneath your feeders.

Finally, remember to wash and rinse birdbaths before refilling them with fresh water. And don't forget to wash your hands after cleaning any bird feeders.

PROTECTING BLUEBIRDS

In an average breeding season, there are billions of resident and migratory birds in North America, and by the end of nesting season, there are billions more. Unfortunately, these numbers belie a real problem—over the past 50 years, extensive studies have shown that bird populations have dropped by around 25 percent continent-wide. Causes include habitat loss, window strikes, pesticide use and predation by housecats.

The majority of threats to birds are associated with people. Collisions with building windows are one of the biggest killers. Nearly a billion birds die each year from flying into windows. During migration through cities, they fly into lit skyscrapers at night. Most small songbirds migrate at night and seem to navigate better in darkness. Businesses in tall buildings are starting to douse their lights during migration, and this has helped.

Collisions with windows also occur at residences. The reflection of sky and trees in windows and glass doors creates the illusion that the flight path is clear. This causes tragic window strikes at our homes. To see bluebirds close-up and protect them, move feeders to within 3–5 feet of window and door glass. This prevents the birds from gaining too much speed on takeoff and reduces impact. Or move your feeders to least 30 feet away from windows to stop collisions due to reflection.

Apply ultraviolet (UV) light reflective stickers to glass so birds can see objects and not reflections. UV stickers are clear and often bird-shaped. We see through them, but the outside reflects UV light, which only the birds can see. There's also a UV light reflective paint that sprays clear on glass but helps birds see the windows.

Studies show that an effective way to reduce window strikes is to hang ¼-inch-thick metallic streamers from the eaves of your house in front of windows. These streamers block the path of bluebirds in flight. There are many more ways to reduce window strikes, so be sure to check online for more solutions.

Before the bird feeding industry was established, it was common to put table scraps outside for the birds to eat. Very few people would waste any food, so often it was just stale bread or tidbits of other old food. However, feeder birds don't accept morsels of this type, and this kind of feeding usually draws critters, such as skunks and raccoons, that are not welcome in backyards. So whether you set out mealworm feeders or put food on cut stumps to attract bluebirds, it is not recommended to use table leftovers to feed them.

According to one study, pesticides are responsible for killing an estimated 72 million birds annually. Most pesticide use is agricultural, but you can support the efforts to reduce the chemical ingestion fatalities of birds in several ways. It's easy to help by purchasing only fruit and vegetables grown locally and in season. Buying only organic fruit and vegetables is another option. You may also decide to go organic in your own garden and backyard. Reducing or eliminating your personal use of pesticides and herbicides will not only make the overall environment safer, but the bluebirds you love will be able to eat uncontaminated wild food as they stage near the feeders in your yard.

About the Author

Naturalist, wildlife photographer and writer Stan
Tekiela is the originator of the popular Backyard
Bird Feeding Guides series that includes *Attracting
& Feeding Woodpeckers*. Stan has authored more than
190 educational books, including field guides, quick
guides, nature books, children's books and more,
presenting many species of animals and plants.

With a Bachelor of Science degree in natural history
from the University of Minnesota and as an active
professional naturalist for more than 30 years, Stan
studies and photographs wildlife throughout the
United States and Canada. He has received national
and regional awards for his books and photographs and
is also a well-known columnist and radio personality.
His syndicated column appears in more than 25 news-
papers, and his wildlife programs are broadcast on a
number of Midwest radio stations. You can follow Stan
on Facebook, Instagram and Twitter, or contact him
via his website, naturesmart.com.